Togethering feels like the transubstantiation of love into language. It astonishes me. It tickles me. It inspires me. It plants a field of sunflowers in my heart then gently beckons that whole glad and gleaming field to join it.

— **Ross Gay**, author of *The Book of (More) Delights*

Lucky for us, in the darkness of our time, Rose Zinnia's marvelous *Togethering* shines a light via spirit and double-blossom and divine hole-y-ness on how not to be desolate, how not to be unskied, despite the dire heaviness, despite that we die. This unpinnable work does not give up— *urgently* does not give up—on the idea that being together and holding together in revolutionary conflagration (the self, the collective, the choir that sings)—is in fact an *activity alive*, one that requires generosity, collaboration, vigilance, and grace. This book is art for the futurity of possibility and being in the flash and whirr without shame, "held together by fragments of delight." Anarchic belonging! Rapturous flight! The invitation is a call to assemble in love!

— **Matt Hart**, author of *Familiar*

Togethering is a voice-rich, matter-of-fact love letter to the self and all selves (un)contained within. The text shapeshifts, queers, and portals into open-hearted, multiplicitous worlds. Rose Zinnia's invented vernacular not only maintains the river of communication with readers, but pulls them closer—a boundaryless, intuitive, exacting acrobatics of language that lifts the fog from around her life-breathing philosophies. I'm grateful for the comfort folded into the many beautiful truths she gifts us, in particular: when the world feels too rigid, linear, commodified, and inaccessible, too cruel to possibly support life, *joy* is imperishably present in all the old hurts, every "exchange of sounds" with friends or strangers, each alchemizing shift of body and water. I would like to follow this poet to her kinder futurepresent.

— **Molly Cross-Blanchard**, author of *Exhibitionist*

Togethering

TOGETHERING — ROSE ZINNIA

PUBLISHED BY LEDGE MULE PRESS
BLOOMINGTON, INDIANA

POETRY / LYRIC ESSAY

FIRST EDITION
SECOND PRINTING, FEBRUARY 2025

COPYRIGHT © 2024 ROSE ZINNIA

CATALOGING-IN PUBLICATION DATA

ZINNIA, ROSE
[POETRY] [LYRIC ESSAY]
[NONFICTION]
[UNITED STATES]
TOGETHERING,
ROSE ZINNIA, PAGES CM—
[FIRST EDITION]

ISBN: 978-0-9993985-7-9

LIBRARY OF CONGRESS CONTROL NUMBER: 2024944868

COVER PAINTING: *VESSEL* BY SHARNAYLA STALER
PAINTING PHOTOGRAPHED BY ANNA POWELL DENTON

EDITED BY DEVON MURPHY

PRINTED ON RECYCLED, ARCHIVAL PAPER ♻

999 999 999 999 999

LEDGE MULE PRESS
415 W. 4TH STREET
BLOOMINGTON, IN 47404

Togethering
Rose Zinnia

LEDGE MULE PRESS

LEDGE MULE PRESS
BLOOMINGTON

Contents

I As In	1
(I Wanted To Die) I Wanted To Stay Alive	2
The World Is Always Ending / We Stay In Love	4
Epistemological	5
Happy Trans Birthday (Nonbinary)	6
Regarding The Impossibility Of The Singular Body	8
My Dental Hygienist Confides In Me	9
Togethering	11
The Gingko, G-d, & Me	31
Tit Vein	33
My Phone Keeps Autocorrecting *Grief* To *Grace*	38
Tendernest	43

✦

Notes, Acknowledgments, & Gratitudes	46

for Wendy, Bloomington, & Kiki

What if we joined our sorrows, I'm saying. I'm saying: What if that is joy?

ROSS GAY

What can one do with a past? What I mean is, what can we do with our bodies?

T. FLEISCHMANN

I As In

i as in sow a muskrat tooth back into jaw
i as in dented pumpkin memory
i as in deflated basketball consciousness
i as in anaphoric internet parrot projection loop
i as in holding uterine lining above a toilet bowl
i as in wide eyed no eyelids whatsoever
i as in anastamosing a dissociated spark
i as in interrogating repression w a single light bulb
i as in carving out swallowed memories from muscle mass
i as in for a purpose beholden but how
i as in flight attendant placing a napkin on your thigh pre-prandial (asmr)
i as in language stripped of signifying mechanisms (earth noises)
i as in adumbrating wolves viewed from a youtube video
i as in plz let me say just one true thing in this form
i as in effortless dwell of complex incorrigible decision
i as in water dressaging across creekstone
i as in every photo of your life stored in a hard drive orbiting earth
i as in swimming like a dog in the riverflesh
i as in choreografted into terrestrial entanglement
i as in twirl-lit in a vague eden
i as in my/our wounds opening like cereus in moonlight
i as in why do people laugh when i interact with them
i as in what if all thoughts even this cannot be untethered from ego
i as in ensconced with a detrimental something
i as in past life as avaricious empress committing sororicide
i as in before you were a human you were black radiance
i as in a golden nothing forever
i as in a trans/cendent immanence
i as in the cracking open sound our reaching toward each other makes
i as in we/us

(I Wanted To Die) I Wanted To Stay Alive

At the same. Time: I wanted to deadhead. & deathbed.
Flashlight in the ever-after. Dreamt of me guffawing on an ordinary

Tuesday. Remembered the light on my face was a whale
song. Wanted to listen for the haptics of our beholding.

Forever. Wanted you to tattoo my name on your jugular. Memorialize
me in vinyl on your rear windshield. Bask in loss like summer. Heat

dissipating. Rewind my momwound. O moonsound: *I wanted, I wanted*.
To die. No, for real. I wanted to end my crimson rivering.

I wanted to de-part. To hear what my name sounded like when I was no longer.
To croon at my funeral. In the most lugubrious key. Eulogize my own vanishing.

I wanted to be future, past, & present. Perfect tenses. I wanted to fall
into the field of spring phemmes. Be topped by a coalition of rootlets.

Summon the cripistemologies of the (un)dead: rot, invisibility, storage units,
copper statues greening. I wanted to inanimalize. To vampire a leaky foxheart.

To grok the holy architecture of beehives. Casually slip into the centralized
heterochromia of a wolf's eye. At the same time. I craved my body on a spit.

My makeup done. Forever. I sought the knot-body hyphally thrumming.
I wanted to be thrust out of the self like a vapor. Locate a moss-fungi

alliance to sublet. To be dispossession. Chimeralish. For just a moment.
The feeling of night silvering into day. I wanted to. Refuse living.

(Regretful.) Hone a pewter seraph to stir me into flame. I wanted to stay
in the womb another ever. To wake into a fuller emptiness. I hungered

to be absence & presence. Technosignature of a prayer. I wanted to be
lain, to be a body laying. To be pellets in fertile loam. The iridescence

on a swallowtail's wing, under a new moon's sclera. To glimmer.
& surrender. To be thirst & the river. & the syllables to sing it.

The World Is Always Ending / We Stay In Love

trans as a devotional (un)state to earthchange

the children we will never have & are always having

the coyote like a bullet in the cemetery at daybreak

tracing back my/our wound we become un/wound

the body a flowering / astonishment as oblation

loss stays merciless / love mercilesser

the sandhill cranes an altar & portal of sky

my/our witnessing bending the letters of *grief* into *grace*

waving evolved out of semaphoring weaponlessness

the body an earth which alchemizes sorrow into wonder

lick me in my/our earth w/hole, hold me/us there g-d

Epistemological

I could have chosen to write this poem about the
drastically-entitled-&-out-of-his-mind-seeming
white septuagenarian who, clearly upset, yowled
I'M ABOUT TO BE UPSET, while turning to address
a line-out-the-door post office like we were attending
his performance art piece, who said he was going to
BLOW UP THE FEDERAL GOVERNMENT because *YOU*
wouldn't give him a money order without proper ID, & I know,
technically, now I have written this poem about him,
but would you please set that aside for the moment
& let me write to you about how you remind me of a babysitter
from my childhood—Alex or Ian, Allison or Marie—telling me a secret
I'm not supposed to know just yet, because of age or subjective cultural
context, in your two-door Honda bumping *let's talk about sex baby*
as I gulp cans of Mr. Pibb in the backseat. You whisper capital-T
truth to me not to gain social capital, nor thwart thine enemy,
nor even to gain my confidence so that one day, in the thick
of an apocalyptic-type emergency, as we likely will be, I will decide
to take you on the proverbial lifeboat above all the others, no,
nor not for any other self-serving reason do you ladle generous
amounts of altruistic, tender, personal attention upon me,
but just for the fact that we are alive together in this moment in time
& space & this post office was once a buffet-style restaurant
where, as a kid, I looked forward to eating the few times a year we did
because this particular establishment had the option to devour
unlimited pizza & soft-serve, which now, you divulge to me,
the guys in the back call this *The Posterosa*, which delights me
which salves me, which allows me to see *we* a little more truly, madly,
deeply, this revealing of our secrets, this dogged bursting through
of taboo, which pamlimpsests our souls a little tighter,
the hidden animals of me on you on me on them
on they on us on me on we.

Happy Trans Birthday (Nonbinary)

We're in my car. Pointing north. *You're nothing,*
you say. *It'll be so easy to come out, because you're—*

nothing. I smile like a sloth at you. I weep
the road in slowmo. So I can: nothing.

You're nothing. You mean it kindly: I'm a cryptid
of taxonomy. But I don't dream. Of becoming. A real some-

thing. No-more. Not a wooden throes-boat. Not the linden
tree Chiron's mother turned herself into after being raped

by Kronus, ashamed her child was a bastard centaur. Sum-thing. A sung-
thing. Sing it with me now: *N-O-T-H-I-N-G.* Wounded-healer. Anymore.

I don't dream. Just animal keen. I swim across the river to you
smashing papayas under the tree line with your hooked hooves.

Butcher phlegmatic. We smear orange on each others' cheeks
till we become pump/kin. It's so quiet I can hear your smile

forming. Cheeks-crinkle. A bleating out the yolkshell.
Yeah: we tender. I lick your teeny nostrils. *My little.*

Nothing. *Your nothing.* Swap eyeball for eyeball. Fall down
the waterfall. For giggles. Walk to Staples in Grand Rapids

where the clerk goes *Have a beautiful afternoon, ladies.* I can't
say it doesn't feel good to be perceived as solely woman. It does.

& it doesn't. *What are you*. When you're nothing? *You're nothing*.
My neighbor uses an iPhone to capture their 12-year-old mowing

the lawn for the first time. They film the whole event, following
the kid around like a doc crew. It's like 45 minutes long, the movie

of this. That's everything. I'm nothing. I must archive my own
annihilated chrysalis. Glean a false tooth from imprinted

memories of monsoons. Take you to my orchid meadow
& let you ladybug all over me. I'll swaddle you even if you

won't real me. Make numb holes of our mouths
until they fall off like lizard tails & we push quarters

into our orificelessness. Hoping for a new theme song to emerge.
One that might coast us back into belonging. Drain all the nuked

milk our e-ghosts' udders can muster. *Yr nothing*.
O girman. O woboy. Make me not a market toy. I was a dart

board. Cactus for you to hang your corpse. I wanted to be a super
mart in the middle of a phantastic emptiness. Open 24. Gleaming.

Packaged. Shrunk. Toilet paper cyborg mummy. The garbage
men I worked with would go, *You look like a girl. Don't let me

get hit by a car, girl. Fucking girl. I've got a wife & kids,
a real life, girl*. Undesirable unthing. *You're nothing*.

At least the grocery store lobsters would honor me
with some dinky ribboned medal that could swing

from my neck like a dented halo. *You're nothing*.
Emblazoned on the back of my jersey. *Happy trans birthday*.

Light limning my as-of-yet milkless breasts.
Another boxcake bedecked with reused candles.

Regarding The Impossibility Of The Singular Body

: genuinely surprised i be/came : transitioning tucked
under skin : i was whimpering psalms of spirit flesh split :

        spilling behallowing hallucinations : dys/integrated
        selves : kicking pebbles round the womb's parking lots :

primed for ⌈immaculate⌉ spectres : to altar me : say *unshame
thyself | decloak the shrouded heart | let the light in-out the wound w/hole* :

o gentle passage i sought : rootlets of seraphins i couldn't
translate : their glossolalia : TLDR; i was hiding in my own corpse

        for warmth : i knew not what loss would survive constant :
        what diminutive self-speck kept dissimulated was ravaging

            'neath my nothingchasm : i knew knot : new togethering : knew
            the riverflesh was sporous : my/our bodies a holy recorder :

        of another bless : an other'd : me in the crumbling sycamore achene :
        this old growth forest of ante-body becoming plural : yes :

            encourage everything's unfurling rot : until i/we spin out of
            my/our felledness : trans/form into resurrections : of coppicing :

My Dental Hygienist Confides In Me

& I in her—at least, as much as I can with my mouth
a cave like this chanting *yuh yuh yuh* every now

& again, some humdrum monk—affirming her confessions—
our eyes two pairs of headlights pouring into each other, a starless

oblivion, below & ahead forever—for I too have a face
patina'd thick with loss's microbiome, too have known addicts

of every degree & desperation, & so can understand her
family, become chosen. She lifts her teal mask

while scraping my enamel of its gunk to make sure
I am hearing her clear. Her eyes crack open like eggs.

I did everything. I could. Her father first, then her little brother,
folded into hushed echoes of their lives, two rot teeth

she couldn't repair or replace. *I still don't know why
it happened. The statistics say two in one family is near*

unprecedented. & I swear: her whispering is in the same
timbre my activist friends & I used when we planned

our direct actions against the state, huddled like owls
in a dinky co-op kitchen, feasting on dumpstered melons

with the dog & the pig & the rats & the cats & the squirrel
who we enlisted in the coming (surely, soon) class war.

& maybe this is why we are here together, now, whispering
about taking your own life under the guise of a tooth preening—

there is nary a day I don't think about my loves & if they will be
here tomorrow. & I too: know shame's wending & distending

of the body, its chiseled scepter piercing into our thrashing
animal. & I too: have sung surreptitiously into the purple twilit

sweetgums' secrets no longer houseable in the little tally
my body makes from the days, built ordinarily of elements,

lest I bloat into shapes I was never meant to stretch into or brave.
In Cleveland, we pulled our bandanas down around our necks—

like she does her mask, now, here—our not-yet-smartphones
wrapped in an afghan outside the room, so the state couldn't listen in

so they couldn't tell us the world we longed for was not possible:
that our trying would never be enough to fill all this ever-metastasizing

loss. Flossing me she says she keeps a recording of her brother
singing on four different hard drives locked up in two separate safes

so she won't ever lose his voice again.

Togethering

AN OBLATION IN TWENTY PARTS

Sometimes I need only to stand wherever I am to be blessed.
—Mary Oliver

:::

The way a lover's hand moves across a kitchen counter: a blue heron grazing the river skin, dipping a toe (paw, talon, hoof, hand) in for the feeling of coolness; the feeling of being touched—held—every once in a while. The river, a launch pad, a slip and slide, a vein in the earthlit skin.

:::

The things we look at when we don't or can't look at each other. That bone-splintered wall. The heart carved into the Black Ash. That Maple leaf freckling with amber. *BILLYBOB LOVES CHARLENE* graffitied on the train trestle. In the song "Sun in an Empty Room" by The Weakerthans, John K. Samson sings about all our almost-intimacies: *The hands that we nearly hold with pennies for the GST / the shoulders we lean our shoulders into on the subway, mutter an apology / the shins that we kick beneath the table, that reflexive cry*. How close we get to holding each other, & how we are, to varying degrees, consciously & unconsciously aware of this, how we simultaneously resist & reify the violence of hyper-individualism in our inadvertent reaching toward each other, in our little sounds & apologies. Via our witnessing, the haptics of the body in varying efflorescences of ongoing apocalypses transform into full-blown intimacies. Accident & apology mutate into recognition of the quotidian tenderness of our collectivity, despite an alienating-by-design system.

:::

Drowning in various animate & psychic griefs, a meme, like the field sparrow's voice, balms me: *last night Ursula K. Le Guin visited my dreams and I said to her "Queerness is a long thread of hurt" and she answered "Now what will you mend with that thread?"*

:::

The next day, another lifesaver: an IRL meme (ie. graffiti), scrawled on a blue dumpster on the B-Line in intricate seafoam green cursive: *EFFERVESCENT FROGS LIVE HERE*. I become the effervescent frog, reading it. I held together by fragments of delight. Apertures to tenderness. Bodies I will never hold, yet do.

:::

Portals are events, quotidian & infrequent alike, that unmask queer holes in our ostensibly indelible totality-reality. Via tenderness, we lilt into each other. Our ways of knowing rupture & our vision resets so we may marvel at the greater mystery of being fractured into distinct, nameable beings, bodies, elements. Every strange connection a euphoric, symphonic oblation to collaboration. An alive-orchestra! We are a witnessing that leaks this collective song. A witness-singing. That numinous possession-like feeling that tilts grief into grace. The words we arrange, too, open portals. Words, like bodies rubbed together, make heat, melt holes in the necropolitical state. We slip through—tingly, effervescent—like dawn frogs in the eddied repositories of creeks, swaddled by the sycamore's roots. Enchanted by the bed light makes. A nest of tenderness. Tendernest.

:::

The time I ran into Ant at the dumpster behind the Little Caesar's. We were both dumpstering for dinner. He had a tall boy of PBR in his front jean jacket pocket, sticking out like a buoy. His jacket an ocean. My body a blur of derealization & substances. There were ten pizzas sitting on the ground beside the trash. (Portals.) A tenderness: the workers kept them separate from, but near, the dumpster, knowing people often came there looking for food. He picked up five, I picked up the other five. We walked back, our foraged cardboard towers blocking our vision, to the forest green, two-bedroom house, where anywhere from ten-to-twelve people also stayed, across from the trap house whose basement had recently exploded. It was expected that if you came over you brought beer or food to share as a kind of tithing. Anyone could drop by whenever they wanted, stay however long they liked. We shoved as many people into that w/hole as possible & played instruments & sang songs & read poems. We did lines, we scoured the carpet for fallen crumbs, we downed stolen space bags & bottles. We were devoted to the next hit. The Health Department came by because our compost pile was too "unruly." We failed each other, & ourselves, often. We were addicts & alcoholics trying to hold on to another day. It was difficult to see the ordinary beauty of earth, but we did, here & there. We cooked meals from dumpstered & donated veggies & served them at the public gazebo by the Cuyahoga River near the bar where all the college kids went. We sat in public & said *Here is some food, will you come talk with us, be with us, without any outright goal besides our togetherness?* One of my childhood heroes, Otto Orf (former goalie for the Cleveland Crunch) stopped by one day & asked me who the leader of our group was (among other things I could have never imagined a childhood idol uttering, such as, *what the hell is tempeh?*) Someone said, *we are non-hierarchical, so there's not really a leader per se. It's more like, we all are just... here. It's more like, this exists & whoever is there is part of it.* Right behind us, the river was teeming, always gushing, a dead dark alive sound. The creak & curling of our rhizomatic, broken weaving.

:::

Togethering *(verb, adverb, noun)* To gather, together. To witness the indelible thread of bodies terraformed through time. A presence beyond this present. A listening beyond linearity. To be held & behold in a devotion of complex relationality. To enshrine our daily caretaking of each other, especially when it is most difficult. *Getting together to figure out how to get together.* The ring we make, eternally. The ante-body of light, the unscripted spiral, the queer portal we forever are.

:::

I ask my dad about my grandma's bipolarity via text as I begin to recognize my own neurodivergence. He says he can't remember much from when he was a kid—he's in his 70's now. He says he probably just thought it was all normal. *She took lithium till she felt good, then stopped, then got drunk & 'accusatory.'* When I was a baby, I am told, she held me. I sucked on her red acrylics. I cooed as she sang to me. With me. The melodies grafting our bodies. I was not yet inculcated into language; I spoke mostly in the argot of the weeping tributary. She comes to me in dreams still, a guide; she speaks in the dialect of laughter.

:::

On the first day of middle school, I was threatened with a truant officer (basically, a cop that forces you to go to school), because I locked myself in my mom's car in the drop-off lot, melting down, crying, screaming, refusing to go in. I did not want to continue living in a world that felt so violent (often in ways I could not express.) When I tried to explain my dysregulation, which I now know was because I was an undiagnosed autistic then, the guidance counselor, chocked it up to me being difficult, to individual failure. He coaxed me out of the car & dragged me toward his office, grasping my tiny forearm with his adult hand, my feet scraping against the pavement, the smooth, squeaky hallways echoing as classmates stared out at the spectacle made of me from their desks. In his office, I bawled for hours as he continuously donned a severely-disappointed-in-me facial expression, shaming me for my "emotional outburst," telling me I would be "ruining" my life if I continued to behave this way. He pointed to an inspirational-style Nike poster on his wall, & read the words on the poster, punctuating each one for effect: *Just. Do. It.* As a late-diagnosed autistic person, I was/am often overwhelmed & disabled by the feeling of having to always be going & doing, performing an ongoingness of production in the way it is supposed to be done for someone (or something) who is demanding it implicitly (& yet, rarely, do I feel as if I am clearly told how it is to be done & am told not to ask questions.) *Go to bed, it's late. Go to work. Just do it. Go off. On god. Time is of the essence. No rest. Do not diverge from the script.* We have essentialized time. Acceptable forms of life imbued with secret codes & checkpoints I struggle to translate. I was taught to loathe my brain, my body, like so many others, for what it could not produce, for what it could not fit into. I have missed many (other people's) deadlines. I have felt so far behind. (Behind what? Where are we heading? Why?) The term deadline originally referred to a line around an open air prison, which would result in death if crossed. We are killing time. Time is a thing that dies.

:::

I was walking with Wendy through the streets of the neighborhood in which we live, holding hands & generally affecting sweetness & love with each other, when a probably 60's-something white guy with a ponytail goes, *Hey kids!* & waves emphatically, grinning at us. Another facial expression I struggled to translate. Wendy thought it was a way to clock us as lesbians. (Edit: after reading this passage to Wendy, she offered another analysis: *Alternatively, perhaps he just didn't know how to address our queerness so veiled it in a general acknowledgment of our "youth" despite us both being 32.*) At the amusement park when I was 11, the age-guesser-person guessed wrong (he said 8) & I won a stuffed, child-sized purple dinosaur filled with tiny Styrofoam pellets I would become fascinated with & often stim between my fingers as I fell asleep. In the Zoom lecture the other day, Robin Wall Kimmerer said that we lose 200 species of beings a day. 200 alphabets of earthlight.

:::

I remember reading Deleuze & Guatarri on a Greyhound when I was 19 & too punk & esoteric for everyone (including myself) &, of the little I understood, they were talking about how revolution—blooming new worlds from the rot of this one—necessarily exists in every moment's happening: an always ongoing element of our relationality. It was me playing with LeTecia's kids in the break room while working the shift at Burger King. The forehead kiss that Andy gave me after I dropped him off at his tent in the woods where he lived next to the river. The unintentional & perfunctory gender-affirming words of a post office clerk early in my transition that relaxed my whole body for the first time in years. The world-altering event thus becomes plural, multivalent—*events*— & is always already extended to the affect & fact of our daily living, our daily loving, our daily, unprescribed devotions to each other. It is a million tiny, unbeknownst, synchronized movements, *small-m*, as Saidiya Hartman has named it. It is our everyday caretaking of each other despite the unending horrors. It is our joy, together, that transgresses. It is our refusal of invisiblized violence, together. It is the hidden sanctuary built of our surviving. & yes, it is, too, the symbolic weight of the police station burning to the ground as we watch, like green auroras emblazoning the black sky. It is the extemporaneous totality of our portal-summoning, our angel-making, through & across time—which is to say, it is our million hands threaded across every sky ever experienced on Earth—it is what we do with our bodies together, in every moment. It is stopping, fully, to really see one another, to really listen. In the Dirty Projectors song "I See You," David Longstreth sings, *I believe the love we made is the art / The projection is fading away / and in its place / I see you.*

:::

The counselors tell me my alcoholism, addiction, mental illness, & neurodivergence have likely been passed down through the family lines. The Internet shows me DNA suspended in fluid, like semen in a toilet bowl. Very few in my family, have been diagnosed (out of fear & stigma & accessibility, I imagine) with anything. Trauma & shame thrive on passed down erasures & silences, epigenetically corralled over centuries. In the respites between the burnouts & meltdowns of my youth, I've wondered if my matter might open & expand into something extravagant, capacious even, if given the chance. It seems to me, more & more, the sorrows & limits we inherit are here to highlight new routes for wonder, despite & in collaboration with the sorrow, the immense, senseless difficulty, which is only made worse for how we treat it. Our brains & bodies, maps to possible worlds (& worlds that were there all along, breathing under the soil, waiting to emerge, like cicadas.) Once, I swear to you, when I was sleeping, wings began to flutter from my shoulder blades, & I saw myself lifting into the sky with the sandhill cranes, the monarchs, the water becoming cloud. Angels all. The body, the portal.

:::

In the tattoo parlor in Cleveland where my cousin works, a family member comes through after work, because she heard I was in town. I ask her about Lucy Rose, my grandmother. *She was a helluva woman, larger than the tiny world offered to her,* she says as my cousin emblazons ink into my finger. *It's like she was bursting out of the seams of her skin. The body could not contain her. Your grandfather though, he did. He controlled her bank account and expenses, he wouldn't let her get a car. All in the name of protection from her mental illness. But she was a highly creative woman. She wrote poems. She felt caged in that house.* It is pervasive & well-documented, this experience for women. When my grandpa was done taking a picture he always said *Good show.* Not to anyone in particular, it seemed, but perhaps to the fact of completing another reference point to the motions, to inscribing a kind of claim over reality's ongoingness. Erasure functions as a mechanism of whiteness, of patriarchy, of all of colonialism's mythologizing taxonomies which mean to sow discord & fear into earth relationalities. It is systematic & drips all over us, & yet—& this lifts me—alterable. It is what we do with our bodies. Together, daily. It is practicing new forms of witnessing the intricacies of the wounds in the collective body. Over the years, I learned to look around for the camera—ideological & actual—that bends & commodifies our seeing into cage, that diminutizes the self into a role, a predictable & inescapable surround that maintains its quiet violence. The flash that relegates the self & its collectivity to outside the realm of the sheerly possible. The lens that surveils & haunts our leaping, that narrows our capacity to witness each other as limbs & roots & fruit in the same body. That shames our practice of seeing beyond the confines of the frame.

:::

Three years ago now, my dead grandma called me by my new name for the first time in a dream, & told me to *get on with it already!* (transitioning), as she laughed freely, puffing smoke from her cigs. In dreams, she shows me my self through her self, lain atop each other like vellum paper. The fact of our necks rubbing, through this palimpsest of time, lain over me, still. She helps me bring our generational traumas to close, with joy, with care, with laughter, with a blasé kind of urgency. She was there when I got sober, whispering & holding me as I convulsed in the bathroom at work. When I cried in my car the millionth time about nothing & everything. When I threw my keys down the storm drain so I wouldn't drive to the liquor store. She wears a crown of phlox on her head. We, two addicts sipping rain above the earth in champagne flutes. She is tall-ish for a woman, like me. Long feet, roomy heart, a mountain range of a person. She rose up, out of the soil, into the earthlight. Our eyes meet level in dreams & spill out crooked rivers. To the sea. To home. I lay supine under an Irish sky & weep as the stars drip & merge with my becoming.

:::

It's difficult to translate the topography of voices I hear in dreams. My dad says there is likely no video or audio recording taken of my grandma's voice before she died, so I have nothing really to compare it with. But in dreams her voice is a dirt road. Mottled with puddles & potholes, yet traversable, carefully. Housing infinite invisible collaborations. She sings, cooing into my ears, made of her ears. Opening like chickweed to light. In mo(u)rning.

:::

I'm feeling sexy & alive & embodied for the first time in my life. Sometimes I just weep, staring at my wrist, my shoulder, the breasts forming on my chest. To have been mostly dissociated into spirit for three decades. & then: to erupt into earthform. We're never final. Complete in incompleteness. Bayo Akomolafe: *God is still being worked out. God is not just an essence, God is a becoming, God is a dying, God is a living. God is the animacy of a mushroom world. God is the weather. God is geology. [...] I like to think about God in this way, as fugitive, as the crack in things that disciplines our attempts to name with any sense of finality.* We, dancing nonlinearly through time. This year of becoming flowers. An anaphoric loop: dying in order to bloom.

:::

My perceptions blend: dreams, waking life, the Internet, crows on the centenarian white oak, sun on a lover's wrist. It all swirls into my ocean-body, integrating. An Instagram comment feels indiscernible from a wolf's call: *I like [calling myself] transsexual because I'm never going to see Lockheed Martin or Amazon or some beer company use it when they pretend to support us.*

:::

After a major poetry website sent out my poem to thousands of e-mail subscribers, I received this comment, not to mention several e-mails instructing me to *PLEASE STOP* using multiple pronouns in my author bio, because it was "confusing & misleading": *What a self-indulgent, breathless rant signifying intellectual failure. Virtually unreadable.* After a few hours of self-hatred, I noticed myself laughing & smiling, thinking about these ten words, because I realized, from a language standpoint, the sentences this stranger took the time to write to me were actually quite pleasurable to read. & then, in nearly the same moment, I saw a comment I failed to see earlier, just above it: *I love this poem.* Yes. I am a breathless rant. I am virtually unreadable, indiscernible, a failure, a misshapen form—yes, yes! Thank g-d! I am in love with the poem I (we) am (are), as I (we) are inexorably both wounded & holy. Sometimes, when my seeing is good, all I notice in this world are hands reaching through the ostensible canyon rift between us, trying to thread. I see your hurt; it is my hurt, too. Our sorrows, weaving palms below the soil. Above the clouds. CAConrad: *It's ALL collaboration. anyone who ever fed you, loved you, anyone who ever made you feel unworthy, stupid, ugly, anyone who made you express doubt or, assuredness, every one of these helped make you. Those who learn to speak with authority to mask their own self-loathing, those may be the deepest influences on us. But they are part of us. And we have each fit together uniquely as a result, and so there are no misshapen forms as all are misshapen forms, from tyrants to wallflowers [...] We are here relying on one another whether or not we wish it.* I want to love everything before I go.

:::

There is a way of moving through the world that is an act of (f)light against the state (of inherited, nihilistic fatalism.) It feels like embodying the uncertainty & improvisational haptics of earth. It feels like refusing the sorrows prescribed us & recognizing a beyond-this-world, an earth beneath the world inscribed atop it, an always already in-this-world being alive. It feels like our bodies remembering their shared enspiritedness, shattered & dispersed into these individualized forms as we are. The ordinary & divine recognition of our collective enfleshment. It feels like togethering our anguish & recognizing the ancient, ceremonial poem we really house in us—in our continued living— this extemporaneous song. The absurd miracle of it all. That we will one day de-part, re-link into water, into new flesh, & that this is abundant reason for worshiping the unlikeliness of our concomitance, here, now. It is the stars translating the sound their dying makes into light, reaching across/through time to plant us here. It is the wind stopping to dance with the cypress arms, then our hands, then the raven's wing—this linking daily lineage of touching, feeling. Polyamorous tendernesses. It is to know: the earth, the trees, the water, are all transcestors. That all of this earth is strangely & beautifully kin. It is to really feel that this earth is queerer than we can imagine. We churn into & out of each other, becoming each other endlessly.

:::

As teenagers at a basement house show in Cleveland, we sat in beer puddles without a sense of futurity. We screamed till our voices ran hoarse: *I see life alive in so many people's eyes / let's hope we won't be dead inside.* We passed out on the concrete floor, our bodies reaching for each other, even then. We were together in a skein of interconnected miseries inherited via our bodies. We practiced a kind of unbeknownst, if naive, witnessing, gleaning songs from all the wounds we couldn't yet fully comprehend. We hurt each other. We tried to love each other in that hurting. When I awoke sober years later from my drunken decade, I remembered everyone I had ever loved & lost, hurt & tried to hold, & it felt as if I had been in a dream, as if the dream was the camera that distended us, as if the warping was itself part of the route to loving a body I couldn't locate for so long. & slowly, I became the oak leaf. I let the loam disintegrate me. & I wept for all the loss—past, still thrumming, & yet to come. Because I knew that we would never stop ending, never stop coppicing from our dying, never stop sorrowing in & out of our selves, again & again, in these portals & attempts to tend to each other's fractures & holes. Which is to say, we are—our living is—the constant practice of remembering our bodies are, inexorably, each other's.

The Gingko, G-d, & Me

*What a hideout, holiness lies spread and borne over
the surface of time and stuff like color.*
—Annie Dillard

Another intractable coven of ever.
Earthlit moonwobbling glittersong.
I lose my name every five

seconds passing. Goldfishing
in my gunnysack. I tread the highways
looking for coywolf corpses to reanimate.

I think sometimes about blowing up
the reactors in the 1990s first-person
shooter computer game *DOOM*,

which is set on the moons of Mars,
& in Hell. Often, the main objective
of any level was to obliterate the level's

infrastructure & get out, alive. I think
of copaganda & my mom's
crush on Bruce Willis.

I think of the Baal Sham Tov saying
*if shells imprison the divine, then all we see
holds holiness.* At the donut shop

a drunken man throws a Diet Coke
into another drunken man's face
after an exchange of sounds

& the perception of their meanings.
It is a miracle moments can be
committed to long-term

memory. Each paused parcel of time,
this one too, with you reader, listener,
an eternity being passed through.

I can't remember my mother's
voice some days. I suck my thumb
straight off in this dank madness.

Will we all be ok, thumbless, like this.
Does this gingko tree acknowledge itself
in/as me. My bank account app asks me to confirm

my identity. I press (1) for *Yes, I am this gingko*.
I touch her (the gingko, g-d, & me) now. I breathe
quickly, directly onto her leafen helm. I kiss

the footprints of every desire path, hoping to pay
off my debts. Forgive me: I give me. What would be
my name if I never stopped unfurling into you?

Tit Vein

FOR WENDY

*Consider that "having" the phallus can be symbolized
by an arm, a tongue, a hand (or two), a knee, a thigh, a pelvic bone,
an array of purposely instrumentalized body-like things.*
—Judith Butler

Judith forgot titties.
—Jackie Wang

blue as wind
shield wiper
fluid, it trembles,
cresting across
the pudgy knoll
of my right
bosom; a pipeline
of blood; the tit vein
wavers in its straightness,
indomitably queer
in its pleasure-desire;
a lightning bolt,
i like to think;
harry potter, but trans;
straight from the heart
to the nipple, a kite string;
it makes me
weep; my heart, my breath,
my chewing, the earth; growing
my tit like this, turning my nipple
puffy & pink; sensitive
& tender; an eye

that cries
milk; a micro
phallus i will press
into u; if u want me to,
after i ask if i can, if
u want that; &
i will take yr breast
in my lips, too, & pull
at the nipple
as if climbing
a rope to g-d;
as if corralling
clouds down from
sky for a bed
for us to lay; as if u are
at the end of a long string
of climbing line i am holding
onto, hanging
down off a cliff
above the sea
where we
have come many times
to remember our itty bitty
ness; our impossible
larger than life ness; now,
it feels like, if i do not pull
hard enough, u will fall &
i will never see u
again; the sea
will swallow u in its
silent teal wash & slush below;
& in the instant
i imagine this tragedy, my hands
no longer perform their hand-
ness; i forget everything
that happened on earth;

how tardigrades look
like mini-elephants
but trunkless; how the light
on the pale green kitchen
counter in morning seemed to
be a god calling my name; &
now, then, i will hurl
my self after u; into that mystic
static below; watching as u
crash into the waves,
a heartbeat before me; hapless;
our bodies will find each other
even then, even there; wash up
on shore together like whales blitzed
w military sonar; or be scavenged
by sharks & shrimp; our skulls
shells for octopuses evading
conger eels; as my lungs fill
w salt & kelp, i will remember
this morning where we walked arm
in arm, laughing, enjoying our to-
gethering, until a cat, all white
ran over, in the road
appeared; a little runnel
of blood, a failed conversation
bubble, trickled down the grey,
grave street; a white minivan
tussled the corpse once more
as we mourned hapless (our bodies
in the surf, churning; the van's
tires, the waves, slashing;
the mouth of the eel, gnawing);
an old man w a terry towel
shaking his head
softly swaddled
the cat, picking them up

as if a delicate cake; the old
woman next door came out,
texted the neighbor whose
cat it was, who came out not knowing
the horror laid before him; just a white
towel on the lawn; a red rivulet
stretching along its hilly
body; the neighbor unable
yet to ascertain death
like this; his skull opened
like a pez dispenser
& out flew spirits who sang
at me, urgently spitting
onto my death-addicted
mind; *let us un-envision*
every possible apocalypse;
let us only imagine
what rollicks w living, what
expands our embrace
of earth; may we become un/wound;
& now i cave; i become w/hole;
in this moment, in every moment;
i hold u; now; tight; tighter; tightest;
i must; in this poem; in this aperture;
i must say it; u are not
falling into the sea
from an impossibly great
height; u are not;
u are entangled w me;
on this bed; this is
here; this is now;
i am jumping
into u; not after u;
i must let u go;
u are a portal
out of linear time's

bleeding & busted fist;
so i hum u; i hum yr
hand in my hand; on my
jawbone; inside of me;
in every future present
past noospheric possible;
we tree; our roots
twist each other;
underground & above;
our branches, arms;
interlaced;
there is nowhere
we are not another

My Phone Keeps Autocorrecting *Grief To Grace*

FOR 3 YEARS AS FLOWERS
AFTER OCEAN VUONG (& ROGER REEVES & FRANK O'HARA)

rose

yr body   once a whisper
dream   elusive as
a scent   absent-presence

slowly   the fiddlehead
fern opens   in april
beneath   the pink moon

tender   as the micro-
biome of yr   finger
nail humming   w becoming
rapture of   lilac
from half-block   away
flash of   orange
monarch   landing
on yr   mustard shirt
in an otherwise   (un)remarkable
indigo morning   yr body an orchestra

the wind   conducts
w the elms   at twilight
can you hear   its for
ever   flesh no

longer   spectre
but   nimbus'd
teeming   w the fox rain

she sprinkles   now
on yr   shoulder

tfftfftfft
fftfftfftff
tfftff
tff

ancient   haptics
spill   from yr
pillowy   cheek
down   the soft
curl   of yr neck
altar   of perforations
reconstruction   site of joy
o holy   intimacy
of water   we/you are
a song   the body
makes of   animacy's
becoming   yes

you   are
finally   & ever
after   sheer
earths   you
the eons of   *no, don't*
slurring into *god, yes*
futurity   cloying back
the ocean's   swell & glisten

i (you) found you (me)

as the   pleiades
tune into   focus
radio station   broadcasting
keens of stars   beyond
we rode in   on comets &
found   ourselves
waking up   in cemeteries
g-d blown   lungs
into   wings

i never   thought
i'd lift   out of my fallow
parking lot   & land
in this   rapturous
anarchic   field gleaming
w congregations   of foxglove
i'd almost   given up
scavenging   abandoned stadiums
of longing   at the end
of the   world

i wasn't only   looking
for you   you too were after
me my/our   future
echo   the promise
of syllables   we'd felt
in dreams   yet couldn't
transcribe   the portals
we made   of my/our listening

this   spell
of   naming
made of   earth

you are flowers

my/our dead   grandma called
my/our name   in the dream

rose

rose

the most   beautiful
part   of your body
is also   where it's
been   how it staggered
thru   days
w only   a heartbeat
lightbeam'd   memory
of a future   shadow

nothing happens too late

i heard you   there
capering   in a wrld
beneath   this one
no longer   hallucination
but   semaphore
trans-ing   time

the earth never abandons us

we   weep
as rain does
here   now—

thank   youtha
nkyouthankyou
thankyouthank
youthankyou
thankyo
u

my phone   keeps
auto   correcting
grief   to *grace*

sometimes   i glide
my hand   up
& down   the angel
my/our   arm makes
for hours   in awe
&   flummox

now   that i can
feel   you
i don't think i could
ever   for
get   how

Tendernest

AFTER CARMEN GIMÉNEZ

The coyotes capering in the creekblood yowl into the night
knowing there is an ear(th) who will catch & sow their ceremony

into the sky's tapestry of listening. My mother dancing
in the car is an ocean breathing luminous fog on the coastal crag.

The nests in which we are transformed to kin, gleaned from the duff
& shive of earthskin, make architectures of relations, ecologies

of care. All our incessant dreaming imprints time onto the blanket
of our softening animal. Every flesh a bluff, a sedge, hurricane—crooked

river where once we rose wet with halos of fire. My daughter,
who will never be & has always been, bears the responsibility

of the moon-violet humus, the continent-shaped cloud, the zinnia weeping
for the gale's long kiss. I swaddle her in throws patina'd with one million

grandmothers—hands, hooves, scales, chlorophylls—tender
with the soft hum of untranslatable dark. There is nowhere

we are not the land. Strumming the wheat, breathing w mosses,
bathing in cloudskin. She calls my/our name, now. Perched in her teal

lawn chair out back below the red-framed window, she is an
estuary of holding. *The spirits are us* & their/our seed is a palimpsest

of centrifuged marrow, a body we've been singing, in one form
& another, into words since before the sequoias even knew

about us, before the chittering cypress groves felt the wind's
clutch, before the mountains rose in cacophonous

harmony with the brightly dying light. Before even,
yes, the lungs learned to long for language.

Notes, Acknowledgments, & Gratitudes

The epigraphs to this book are from Ross Gay's *The Book of Delights* & T. Fleischmann's *Time Is The Thing A Body Moves Through*.

Epistemological

This poem is dedicated to the post office workers at the Post Office on Walnut Street, in Bloomington, Indiana, which I frequented weekly for many years & still think about & miss.

My Dental Hygienist Confides In Me

The line "the little tally my body makes of the days, built ordinarily of the elements" owes homage to John Donne's "Holy Sonnets," specifically the line "I am a little world made cunningly / Of elements and an angelic sprite." This poem is dedicated to all of my friends in Kent, Ohio c. 2008-9, as well as all the animals who lived with us at the co-op house. Special shout out to our sweet pig, Officer Squiggly, who rooted me joyfully awake daily & also often gave me love bites/kisses, one of which left a divot-scar on my nose, which is still visible to this day.

The Gingko, G-d, & Me

The epigraph is from Annie Dillard's book *For The Time Being*.

Togethering

This lyric essay is dedicated to Ross Gay, who has taught me so much about love, about joy, about loss—which is to say—so much about everything.

p. 11: The epigraph is from Mary Oliver's poem "It Was Early."

p. 14: The italicized quote is a tweet by @sagescrittore on 25 October 2021.

p. 17: The italicized quote is a variation of a quote by Fred Moten from his essay "the plan" published at *The Poetry Foundation* blog, 10 January 2010.

p. 19: Gratitude is owed to Jeff at Hart Farms in Bloomington for teaching me the etymology of the word "deadline" one early Fall morning as we drank coffee & looked out on a field of strawflowers opening in the misty morning sun.

p. 21: The Saidiya Hartman book referenced is *Wayward Lives, Beautiful Experiments: Intimate Histories of Riotous Black Girls, Troublesome Women, and Queer Radicals*.

p. 26: The italicized quote is from Bayo Akomolafe's interview with *For The Wild* titled "On Coming Alive to the Senses," 17 August 2022.

p. 27: The italicized quote is an Instagram comment made by @chirp.chirp.boom (unknown date, c. summer 2021).

p. 28: The italicized quote is from CAConrad's "The Right to Manifest Manifesto" from *A Beautiful Marsupial Afternoon*.

p. 30: The italicized quote is from the song "My Bedroom Is Like For Artists" by Latterman.

Tit Vein

The epigraphs are from Judith Butler's essay "The Lesbian Phallus and the Morphological Imaginary" & Jackie Wang's essay/zine *The Phallic Titty Manifesto*.

Tendernest

This poem is after Carmen Giminez's poem "Only a Shadow" from *Be Recorder*. It was originally commissioned by matthew anthony batty & Rachel De Cuba as an ekphrastic for their art show *My Daughter Gathers Seeds* in Greenville, SC in 2022.

My Phone Keeps Autocorrecting *Grief* to *Grace*

This poem is after Ocean Vuong's "Someday I'll Love Ocean Vuong," which is after Roger Reeve's "Someday I'll Love Roger Reeves," which is after Frank O'Hara.

My thorough & embodied gratitude to the publications that originally published the following poems from this chapbook, some with slight variations:

Peach Mag: "I As In" & "Happy Trans Birthday (Nonbinary)"

Academy of American Poets (Poem-A-Day): "Epistemological"

SOLID STATE: "The Gingko, G-d, & Me"

Foglifter Journal: "The World is Always Ending / We Stay in Love"

New Ohio Review: "My Dental Hygienist Confides in Me" (Finalist for the 2024 *NOR* Award, judged by Naomi Shihab Nye.)

like a field: "Tendernest" & "Tit Vein"

There are SO many people (& beings, spirits, flowers, trees, networks beneath the soil, animals, wind currents, planetary alignments, et al) who made this book possible—who make every day living, seeing, & breathing, realized. It was in constant collaboration that I made these poems, & they, me. There is a long, impossible list of inimitable artists, poets, writers, musicians, & creatives who my work is made of & from. You make me want to make more beautiful things, & I've felt less alone knowing we are divinely connected & collaborating even when not in direct communication. Every single little moment. Every portal we open. Every sentence against the sentencing. My poems are collaborations across time. That it is wholly impossible to ever make a book by one's self, to claim a thing as solely "mine"—how blessed.

Wendy, my dear one: this chapbook is for you & everything we've shared, gathered, & grown! So much of my life & writing is because of & has been in constant witness by you—has happened alongside & with you & is a result of our concomitant relationality. So many of these poems carry your vision, your care, your love, like a seed in them. I'm so lucky for the love & growth & life we've shared through all the years. Your presence alongside me throughout so much of this life has been nothing short of miraculous & beautiful. Grateful beyond language ♡

Ross: our collaboration & friendship has bloomed me into forms & ways I wasn't able to even conceive of prior. I think we have often said this to each other: your voice is all up in my voice—your love, your laugh, your sorrow, your joy!—entangled with mine.

How lucky!!! You are a deep soul friend. Thank you for nurturing & being a beacon for my work over the past twelve (!) years. I feel as if I am always in the garden with you, loving on this earth, & each other.

To all the sweeties from the MFA program (and beyond) at Indiana University—past, present, profs, my students, peers—too many to fully name, how blessed—where many of these poems were tenderly boosted into their next (more expansive) forms: our gathering was beyond special. Your insights surely made my work evolve, needfully so, including many of the poems & essay in this chapbook. Our conversations, potlucks, workshops, walks, gardenings, & overall togethering lives on in my body, tenderly. Jay: our chats in your seminars forever shifted me & my poetics & vision into the realm of the vast & sheerly possible. Adrian: your clear vision, editorial prowess, & deep understanding of poetics helped me understand my own relationship to lucidity & communication in poems more vitally & wholly, for which I am ever grateful—thank you! Cathy, Stacey, Romayne: the mentorship & care you offered me is still so cherished. To all my students over the years: why are y'all so cool though?? What a gift to have been in relationship with you. You changed my writing for the better.

Bella & Michelle: my work works because of all we shared as emerging writers making our way in little Bloomington. So many years of caring for each other's writing. All the time & reading(s) & tours—& & &—that we shared. What a wonder to be beheld by/with you, to have grown alongside you. I miss you daily.

Everyone who ever was a nutrient in the vast root system of Monster House Press & w the trees in Columbus & Bloomington: growing & birthing books & community with you over that decade or so altered/altared me, taught me how to bloom, showed me how to co-build the worlds we want to see. There is no way I'd have become who I am today, no way I'd have written these poems, without experiencing all that we shared. Thank you for all.

Bloomington friends, loves, dears: it is an astonishment to be co-made because of a place, its people, its land & water. I became so much with you & miss you all the time. Thank you for holding me/us.

To all the queer, trans, nonbinary, Two-Spirit, and genderqueer/non-conforming angels I've had the joy of being in community (corporeally & spiritually) with—past, present, and future: I write with you. Your living swaddles me, like prayer. I'm grateful to be creating a more expansive & possible futurity with you. Special shout out to the divine transsexual crew I met at Banff Centre during a fiction residency—Casey, Nolan (NN), Shannon, & Coop. I love you all & our conversations meant so much to me.

To all my autistic, ADHD, neurodivergent, disabled, & addict babes: I love you. Our brains are maps to new worlds. I'm so glad you exist. I write with you.

Dave & Ross & Kayte at Ledge Mule Press: thank you for believing in this book & wanting to publish it! Being in literary community with you in Bloomington over the years has been so joy-inducing.

Biff: fellow earth sun angel. Your love is so big & so real. The ways you inspire me & hold me & see me. Much of the way I have leaned into Spirit is because of our togetherness. Thank you for who & how you are in this earth.

Molly (Cross-B): also my fellow earth sun angel. O that our paths crossed in this life even! How lucky. Thank you for your generous eye & flattering words. I'm so glad for the miracle of having met you in this life.

Sharnayla: & yet another fellow earth sun angel. Thank you for the gorgeous cover painting & all the tattoos & love over the years in Bloomington—you've literally helped make me beautiful, inside & out. I'm so grateful for your heart & soul. Thank you Anna, for photographing the cover painting, & all the friendship & photoshoots we've shared over the years! & thanks to Bryant & Lauren, who own the painting which graces this cover, for permission to use it.

Matt: thank you for all your support & kindness with these poems, & over the years! It has been so lucky to meet you & get to be in literary community & friendship with you.

To my Dad, Mom, Erin, & Dean: I consider myself very lucky to have your support & love throughout my life. I am buoyed by your care. Thank you for being such a loving family who is always committed to witnessing each other's change with love.

Rachel & matthew: thank you for commissioning me to write "Tendernest." Our collaborations & friendship over the years in Bloomington meant a lot to me.

Thank you to everyone who has ever solicited my writing, asked me for poems, came to a reading / spoke to me after, & supported my work in general: you mean so much to me!!

To my grandmother, Lucy Rose: I know you're with me, even though you're departed. I can still feel you holding me, after all these years. Thank you for always showing me the way through. & for roasting me to shreds in dreams LOL.

My Devy: the gem in my ear, my bunny, editor exemplar! O this book would not be nearly as tight & clean & beautiful as it is without your good eyes! To be witnessed & loved by you is a balm & sweetness I cherish deeply. Your support, your heart, your seeing. I tear up thinking about it. Life is immensely more beautiful, more blessed, more funny, more joyful alongside you. Whatever spirits brought us together, I owe them a major debt. Loving you is a luckiness, ease, & wonder. I love you so much!!!

To Spirit, g-d, the earth: I am gratefully a part of you. So beyond joy for that. You taught me so much about how to be. Every thought a thought of/with/for/because of you.